Edward Roberts and the Story of the Personal Computer

Susan Zannos

Mitchell Lane
PUBLISHERS

PO Box 619 • Bear, Delaware 19701
www.mitchelllane.com

Unlocking the Secrets of Science

Profiling 20th Century Achievers in Science, Medicine, and Technology

Edward Roberts and the Story of the Personal Computer

Printing   1   2   3   4   5   6   7   8   9   10
Library of Congress Cataloging-in-Publication Data
Zannos, Susan.
     Edward Roberts and the story of the personal computer/Susan Zannos.
          p. cm. — (Unlocking the secrets of science)
Summary: Describes the life and work of the man credited with being the first to design and market a personal computer.
Includes bibliographical references and index.
     ISBN 1-58415-118-8 (lib.)
     1. Roberts, Edward, 1941- —Juvenile literature. 2. Computer engineers—United States—Biography—Juvenile literature. [1. Roberts, Edward, 1941- 2. Computer engineers.] I. Title. II. Series.
     QA76.2.R63 Z36 2002
     621.39'092—dc21   2002070257

ABOUT THE AUTHOR: Susan Zannos has been a lifelong educator, having taught at all levels, from preschool to college, in Mexico, Greece, Italy, Russia, and Lithuania, as well as in the United States. She has published a mystery *Trust the Liar* (Walker and Co.) and *Human Types: Essence and the Enneagram* was published by Samuel Weiser in 1997. She has written several books for children, including *Paula Abdul* and *Cesar Chavez* (Mitchell Lane). Susan lives in Oxnard, California. For this story, Susan personally interviewed Ed Roberts and he has approved this story for print.

PHOTO CREDITS: cover: Spencer Smith; p. 6 Spencer Smith; p. 8 Corbis; p. 11 Karsten Thielker/AP Photos; p. 14 Spencer Smith; p. 16 Barbara Marvis; pp. 17, 19, 20 Corbis; p. 22 AP Photo; p. 24 Corbis; p. 30 Al Luckow; p. 36 Corbis; pp. 38, 43 Spencer Smith

PUBLISHER'S NOTE: In selecting those persons to be profiled in this series, we first attempted to identify the most notable accomplishments of the 20th century in science, medicine, and technology. When we were done, we noted a serious deficiency in the inclusion of women. For the greater part of the 20th century science, medicine, and technology were male-dominated fields. In many cases, the contributions of women went unrecognized. Women have tried for years to be included in these areas, and in many cases, women worked side by side with men who took credit for their ideas and discoveries. Even as we move forward into the 21st century, we find women still sadly underrepresented. It is not an oversight, therefore, that we profiled mostly male achievers. Information simply does not exist to include a fair selection of women.

Contents

Ed Roberts is shown here with the electronic calculator he designed. It was offered for sale in 1972 and he sold thousands of them.

Chapter 1

Computers

• •

Ed Roberts is widely accepted as being the man who first designed and marketed the personal computer. He did this, in the early 1970s, because he stubbornly believed that ordinary people would want to own their own computers if they could afford them. All the experts assured him that he was wrong, that the effort to build an inexpensive general-purpose computer would fail for lack of public interest.

By the time Ed Roberts was born in 1941, the development of large, expensive computers was well under way. Necessity mothered most, if not all, of the developments that created the computers we have now. Even the word *computer* is an historical accident caused by the earliest needs that these amazing machines responded to. It could as well be called a communicator or an organizer or any of probably dozens of other names related to the many functions that computers perform.

An example of a pressing necessity in computing was the U.S. Census Bureau's job of counting all the people in the country every 10 years. The information from the 1880 census took over seven years to process, done mostly by hand. As 1890 approached, people at the census bureau faced the nightmare possibility of not being able to count the rapidly increasing population (immigrants were pouring into the U.S. from all over the world) before it was time for the 1900 census.

An inventor and engineer named Herman Hollerith, who was working for the census office in Washington, D.C.,

Herman Hollerith used the punch card system to develop tabulating machines for the United States Bureau of Census. In 1911, he sold his Tabulating Machine Company to the Computing-Tabulating-Recording Company, which in 1924 became International Business Machines (IBM).

designed a machine that counted and sorted information that was punched into cards. Census workers went all over the country, to every person, and asked questions about their age, education, and living conditions. The information was punched into cards with a keyboard punch, and the cards were fed into Hollerith's machine. The machine passed pins through the holes and into mercury cups that completed an electrical circuit. Then the machine sorted the cards into categories, and a counter totaled up the number of cards in each category.

In less than one year, on December 12, 1890, the census office was able to report that there were 62,947,714 people in the United States, and how many of these people were men and how many were women, what their level of education was, and many other facts about the population. Many countries purchased this tabulating machine to use in census taking. Hollerith sold his Tabulating Machine Company in 1911 to a company called the Computing-Tabulating-Recording (CTR) Company, which in 1924 changed its name to International Business Machines, or IBM.

A dozen years later, in Germany in 1936, a civil engineering student named Konrad Zuse was trying to develop an automatic computing machine for the very good reason that he hated having to solve the difficult calculations his studies required. As he confided in an interview recorded for the London Science Museum in 1975, "You could say that I was too lazy to calculate, so I invented the computer."

Since he knew almost nothing about the calculating machines that had already been developed, he didn't waste time imitating other people's methods. Up until Zuse's time, all the calculators had used our traditional 10 digits, 0 through 9. Zuse figured that simpler is better. He decided to use the binary system, the simplest number system possible because it has only two numbers, 0 and 1. This meant that he could use a switch, because a switch has only two positions, on and off.

Any number that can be counted in the decimal system (using the digits 0–9) can be counted in the binary system. For example, the number one is 1. The number two is 10, or one two and no ones. The number three is 11, one two plus one one. The number four is 100, one four, no twos, and no ones. Five is 101, a four and a one. Six is 110, four plus two. Seven is 111, four plus two plus one. Eight is 1000. And so forth. Any decimal number (or any other kind of number for that matter) can be represented by a string of 1s and 0s.

Zuse's first successfully operating machine used the telephone relay, an electromechanical device that had two states, on and off. It used 2,600 of these relays and could add, subtract, divide, multiply, find square roots, and convert decimals to binary numbers or vice versa. But it was slow. A friend suggested that vacuum tubes would speed things up because the switching would be done by electrons jumping millions of times a second rather than by movable mechanical relays. The speed would then be a thousand times faster than that of Zuse's existing machine. Zuse asked the German government to finance his project, so Germany came very close to being the first to develop a digital electronic computer. But before the theory could be put into practice, Germany was losing World War II and had no resources to put into the development of such a machine.

At the same time that Konrad Zuse was avoiding his homework in Germany, a mathematician named Alan Turing in England was wondering whether a machine could be designed that would be able to perform any mathematical process. Up until that time the term *computer* referred only to the people who did calculations by taking the numbers they were given and processing them with their brains and writing down the results. Turing wondered whether a machine could do the same thing: take numbers and then follow instructions and come up with other numbers.

Turing realized that if such a machine could do this with numbers, it could do the same thing with any symbol. It could work with letters. It could work with other visual images. It could manipulate any kind of symbols for which it was given both the symbols and the instructions it needed to follow. For example, if the symbols the machine was given were a list of words, it could be given instructions for several different ways of organizing the words. It could arrange them alphabetically (if the alphabet were provided in the instructions it was given). It could arrange them according to the number of letters in the words, or put them in groups that contained specific combinations of letters.

Alan Turing wasn't at all interested in actually building such a machine; he was only interested in logical theory. But during World War II some people in Britain were very interested indeed in finding out if Turing's machine could be built. These people were code-breakers who had the task

Konrad Zuse, shown here, is known as the "Father of the Digital Computer." He was a German engineer who designed the first freely programmable, fully automatic computer in 1941, known as the Z3. The original computer was destroyed in bombing raids during World War II. Zuse died in 1995.

of deciphering the codes used by Germans in the secret transmissions that told when and where Germany would bomb England. They needed a machine that could take input symbols—the coded messages—and convert them to output symbols—the original messages in German.

Like Zuse's friend in Germany, an engineer in England named Tommy Flowers realized that in order for the Turing machine to operate rapidly enough, it would have to use vacuum tubes rather than electromechanical switches. The resulting machine, called the Colossus because of its enormous size, was completed in December of 1943 and tested with a problem that had taken several days for the human code-breakers to solve. Colossus solved the problem in 30 minutes. Colossus had computed letters rather than numbers, demonstrating that computers could transform symbols of any kind according to a given set of rules.

The United States also had a problem that desperately needed to be solved during World War II. The Ballistics Research Laboratory (BRL) in Maryland needed to figure out the angles at which the barrels of large guns needed to be aimed into the air for their shells to hit the intended target. The trajectories, or curves the shells would travel in, would need to change according to the distance of the target, the weight of the shell, how hard the wind was blowing, and many other factors. The laboratory had to produce booklets with tables that gave the correct settings for thousands of trajectories for each gun. The calculations for each trajectory took a human being with a desk calculator several days to compute.

As the war intensified, the BRL fell further and further behind and the gunners didn't have the information they needed. The BRL knew about the high-speed calculations that could be accomplished with vacuum tubes, so they commissioned the development of the ENIAC, Electronic Numerical Integrator and Computer. The ENIAC was nearly 100 feet long, 8 feet high, 3 feet deep and weighed 30 tons. It had 18,000 vacuum tubes, 70,000 resistors, 10,000 capacitors, 6,000 switches, and 1,500 relays. It cost nearly $500,000. It could perform 5,000 additions per second, 357 multiplications per second, and 38 divisions per second. The war was over before the ENIAC was completed in November 1945, but it demonstrated that large electronic systems could be built.

The enormous size and cost of Colossus, ENIAC, and the other huge computers that soon followed convinced the business world that only governments, scientific research labs, large universities, and huge corporations would have a use for computers. As Ed Roberts was growing up, he knew that at least one person would like to have a computer of his own. He would.

In the early days of computers, they were very large and expensive and took up a lot of space. This is a UNIVAC Mainframe in 1954 that consisted of (left to right) an oscilloscope, the supervisory control panel, external memory tape machines, and in the background, the central computer.

Though Ed Roberts was born in Miami, Florida, his mother took him back to Wheeler County, Georgia during World War II while his father was in the Army.

Chapter 2

Early Years

Ed Roberts was born in Miami, Florida, in 1941. Both of his parents were from Georgia and had moved to Florida in the late 1930s. Roberts says, "Most of Georgia left at the end of the Depression to move south, move to Miami. That was sort of the land of promise, like people from the Midwest going out to California." His father, Henry Melvin Roberts, was an appliance repairman who eventually owned his own business in Miami. His mother, Edna Wilcher Roberts, was a housewife. A younger sister, Cheryl, was born after World War II.

During and after World War II, while his father was in the army in Germany, Ed's mother took him back to Georgia, to her parents' farm in Wheeler County. Henry and Lillian Wilcher raised cotton, corn, and watermelon and had some cows and hogs. "These were real small farms," Roberts remembers, "hundred-acre kinds of farms. I can remember when they got water out of a well. Actually with a bucket. I think they got electricity in the late 1940s when the REA got into this area." (The REA was the Rural Electrification Agency of the federal government.)

When Ed's father came back from Europe, the family returned to Miami, but Ed continued to spend his summers in rural Georgia until he was in his last years of high school. His mother's family was large, with six children, and well established in Wheeler County. "One of the nice things about a rural area," Ed Roberts says, "and I think about this—everybody is important in a small town. You're not anonymous. In a city—and I was raised in the city—nobody

Miami, Florida was the land of promise toward the end of the Great Depression.

knew if you were there or not. Nobody cared if you were there or not. And you really developed the idea that you were sort of anonymous. But in a small town, you're not. You do anything . . . it's all over town. And that's true of almost everybody. So everybody feels that they're important. It gives you a feeling of worth that you don't really get when you live in a city."

So in the 1940s and early 1950s, while the long warm summers of Wheeler County, Georgia, were ripening the corn and the watermelons, they were also ripening a boy's sense of his own worth, his trust in his own judgment. He developed the belief that he could do whatever he set out to do. Ed Roberts took this belief with him back to Miami when the school years began each fall. He was interested in electronics, and he actually built relay computers when he was still in high school. Relays are basically on and off devices. He realized that anything that could be done with digital electronics, such as calculators, could be done with relays.

In his senior year in high school, Ed got into a special program in which the students left school at noon and worked in research programs. The program he worked in was experimental surgery at the University of Miami. Ed planned to become a doctor, and he continued to work in experimental surgery even after his first year of college at Miami, where he did surgery in the dog lab. "I was always intrigued by medicine," Roberts says. "I was particularly intrigued by the science of medicine at that time. I was involved with the heart-lung machine development. At that time it was a new thing; there were only a couple of places in the country that were doing open-heart surgery with heart-lung machines, and Miami was one of them. I worked with a doctor who was doing that. I did a good bit of surgery in the dog lab using the heart-lung machine. We would use it in the same way as with human patients."

It did not seem extraordinary to the 18- and 19-year-old Ed Roberts to be doing open-heart surgery. It was interesting, and he had the opportunity, so he did it. He was working with a neurosurgeon who shared his interest in electronics. They used a lot of electronic instrumentation

This is a heart-lung machine developed by John Osborn of Stanford University in the 1950s. Ed Roberts was privileged to be able to experiment with such a machine in the dog lab where he worked at the University of Miami.

in the lab. The surgeon said, "What you ought to do is change your major from biology to engineering or physics, and that will make you unusual going to medical school. Once you get out of medical school, you'll never have the time to study this stuff, so you've got to do it before you go to medical school." The neurosurgeon's advice seemed reasonable to Ed. His intention was still to go to medical school, but he changed his major to electrical engineering while he was at the University of Miami.

In 1962, before he was quite 21 years old, Ed Roberts married Joan, a Miami girl. When Joan became pregnant, he was delighted to be starting a family, but he was also at a loss as to how he would support a wife and child and still continue his education. He found out about a program in the U.S. Air Force that would pay for college. He enlisted in May of 1962 with the intention of getting into the Airman Education and Commissioning Program.

Once in the Air Force, however, Ed found out that it took about six to eight months to get into the program. Meanwhile, he had been selected to go to a yearlong electronics school. He decided to start that course and then apply for college while he was taking it. But it turned out that once he was in electronics school, he wasn't able to apply for the college program because he hadn't yet reached a certain skill level. It was rather like the fairy tale in which the hero must repeatedly turn aside from his quest in order to complete various other tasks along the way. And as in the fairy tale, it turned out that each of the tasks was a necessary preparation for the completion of the quest.

Ed Roberts went through his basic training in San Antonio, Texas, went to tech school in San Antonio, and taught electronics at Lackland Air Force Base in San Antonio. His first son, Melvin, was born there in early 1963. His second son, Clark, arrived in 1964, and David in 1965. Also in 1965, Roberts finally got into the college program he had been waiting for, at Oklahoma State University in Stillwater, Oklahoma.

Roberts describes OSU as a very forward-thinking school, particularly when it came to computers: "Believe it or not, they had an IBM 1620 in an open lab. No one monitored the machine. This was a big machine with a lot of money invested into it. It was open to engineering students and we would go down there and just put our name on a roster to use it. It was fantastic! And that had probably more impact on my feelings later on about computers than anything else." After his experiences working on the computer at Oklahoma State, no one was going to be able to tell Ed Roberts that individuals would have no use for a computer.

Once he received his electrical engineering degree from Oklahoma State University in 1968, and his commission as

In the early 1960s, Ed Roberts taught electronics at Lackland Air Force Base in San Antonio, Texas. This photo, taken at Lackland AFB, shows a student from the Combat Control School during a medical exercise.

an officer in the U.S. Air Force, Roberts had a four-year commitment to the Air Force. He was transferred to the special weapons laboratory in Albuquerque, New Mexico, where he was a research officer. While there he designed the first fire-control system for laser weapons. Fire control is the system that aims and fires weapons. These were the first laser weapons ever designed, and they were completed on a research basis, not for production. Roberts went to Albuquerque as a second lieutenant and left the Air Force in 1972 with the rank of captain.

This was during the Vietnam War, when there was violent dissent within the United States about our involvement in Southeast Asia. "It was a very interesting period," Ed Roberts remembers. "I would travel around the country, checking on different things when I was working as a research officer. If I were wearing a uniform I could guarantee that if I went through a major airport somewhere, people would spit. I was never spit on, but I was spit at, and I was called 'baby killer' and stuff like that. It was a bad

Vietnam was a controversial war and many Americans opposed our involvement there. Ed Roberts was in the military then and he thought of himself as very patriotic. This photo was taken during fighting on "Hamburger Hill" in the Vietnam War.

period. Those of us who were in the military at that time were really trying . . . we thought of ourselves as being patriotic and doing something for the country. And we were really pretty badly treated by a good percentage of the civilian population. It was a pretty unfair period. We were blamed for all the bad things in the world. If you had a uniform on, you were responsible for anything bad that happened in the world. That was sort of the mentality."

The young people who opposed the Vietnam War, and who fought for civil rights and individual freedom during the turbulent years of the 1960s and early 1970s, imagined that they were taking part in a revolution that would change the country and the world. They were right about one thing: there was a revolution about to take place that would change the world. But it wasn't the political revolution they thought would happen. It was a technological revolution, and it would break out in Albuquerque, New Mexico.

Bill Gates today is the billionaire CEO of Microsoft, a company he co-founded with Paul Allen. Gates and Allen were briefly employed by Ed Roberts in the 1970s.

Chapter 3

Freedom Fighters

● ●

Up until 1970 there were basically two kinds of computers. There were huge room-sized computers, called mainframes, which were made by IBM and other big companies. They cost hundreds of thousands of dollars and could be purchased only by governments or huge corporations. The other kind of computers were called minicomputers, but they were mini, which means "small," only in relation to the enormous mainframe computers. They were still pretty big and very expensive. These were purchased by universities, scientific laboratories, and large businesses. Businessmen who ran the companies that made computers believed that ordinary people would have no use for a computer.

The reason for this misconception was that not only were there two kinds of computers, there were also two kinds of computer users. The first kind of users were the people who actually operated the big expensive computers to solve the problems that professors and scientists and businessmen wanted to have solved. For example, a chemistry professor might be working on a problem related to the number of electrons in a molecule of a particular element. The professor would have the information punched into cards and the cards delivered to the computer operator, who would run the program and return the results to the professor. These computer operators were the official computer establishment.

The second type of computer user was not official. All across the country there were kids who were doing anything they could to get their hands on computers the way Ed Roberts had had a chance to do at Oklahoma State University.

In Seattle, 15-year-old Paul Allen and 13-year-old Bill Gates rode their bikes after school every day to a company, Computer Center Corporation, that let them find errors in the Digital Equipment Corporation computer's programming. CCC had a contract that stipulated that as long as there were errors found in the DEC programs, the company didn't have to pay DEC for using the computer. The kids were saving the company money. Eventually they even got paid a little for their efforts. Allen and Gates knew how lucky they were—very few kids their age had even seen a computer, much less actually worked on one.

At Massachusetts Institute of Technology (MIT) in Boston, some of the freshmen spent so many nights prowling the halls of Building 26, where the $3-million TX-0 computer was housed in the second-floor Research Laboratory of Electronics, that they never made it to classes. And why? Because sometimes in the middle of the night, official users

Paul Allen, left, with Bill Gates, shortly after they founded Microsoft in the late 1970s.

who had signed up to use the computer would sleep in and not show up. This meant that the kids could actually get their hands on the computer for an hour or two. What was it they wanted to do? That was exactly what separated them from the official users with practical programs. They didn't have any aim beyond finding out what the computer could do. And they came up with things it could do that the official users had never dreamed of.

In Sunnyvale, California, Homestead High School electronics teacher John McCullum noted that one of his students needed more of a challenge, so he arranged for the boy, Steve Wozniak, to visit nearby Sylvania Electronics to use their computers. Steve was particularly enchanted with a Digital Equipment Corporation minicomputer. He read the manual and began designing his own computer. He knew that he would design computers someday, and he was right. He would eventually be one of the founders of Apple Computer Company. Kids like Steve had grown up around electronic technology and were not intimidated by it. But at that time, 1969, it was almost unthinkable for an individual to own a computer.

Almost unthinkable, but not quite. In Albuquerque, New Mexico, Ed Roberts was thinking about it. After Lieutenant Roberts got his family settled in Albuquerque in 1968 and started work at the Air Force special weapons lab, he and two other officers started a business in his garage. The business was originally started to produce telemetry equipment for model rockets. The name of the company was Micro Instrumentation Telemetry Systems, or MITS.

"We didn't make a lot of money," Roberts says, "probably didn't make any money . . . but we got a lot of experience. There's always a lot of excitement in design work, in designing electronic devices or engineering devices. There's a creative excitement associated with that that I suspect is like writing or painting, or anything else you do that's creative. As a matter of fact I consider engineering to be the ultimate creative form."

Roberts' creative energies were soon casting about for other electronic devices to design. One was an optical communicator that did quite well. Two or three other things didn't do so well. The three partners wrote some articles for the magazine *Popular Electronics,* which was the periodical that most of the electronic hobbyists in the country read. Ed was working on an electronic calculator, but his partners said they didn't think there was any market for it. He bought them out and had the company to himself for about six months. Then he sold 15 percent of it to Bill Yates, who remained his partner through the entire explosive history of MITS.

The two of them finished the calculator design and put it on the market early in 1972. There was a cover article about it in *Popular Electronics.* They sold thousands of them. "It was really the first personal computer," Roberts says. "The calculator was set up so that you could add a programmer to it and write programs and control the calculator externally with a programming box, and you really had a full-blown real-world computer. Not a very potent computer, but you had a computer."

The machine had hundreds of transistors and resistors and discrete circuits and capacitors, plus some large integrated circuits. It had its own set of calculator chips that were made by a company called EAI. It was a relatively complex design compared to calculators now. By 1973 calculators had been simplified to the point where they could be produced with just a soldering iron. Ed Roberts went downtown in Albuquerque and bought a calculator for less than the materials cost MITS—and it was similar to the ones they were producing.

"I thought there was something we didn't understand," Roberts says. "But it turned out we understood it and these other companies were building machines for less than their cost and they all went bankrupt. Everybody that was in the calculator business went bankrupt. That was the problem. There were so many people in it, and it got to be such a simple device to make, there was just no way to make any money."

In the spring of 1974, Ed Roberts went to the offices of *Popular Electronics* and talked to two of the editors, technical editor Les Solomon and editorial director Arthur Salsberg, about a computer project they had going at MITS. Salsberg agreed to do an article about the project if MITS could produce a machine that would work, and if they could keep the cost under $400. "But it had to be a real general-purpose computer," Roberts says, "not just a box with lights on it. And that's what we did."

In order for such a feat to be conceivable, much less actually possible, an astonishing progression of technological developments had occurred in the previous 25 years. Two of these technological breakthroughs were key. The first was the development of the transistor. The transistor is a crystal in which small flows of electrons can be controlled to provide signals. Crystals of very pure silicon proved to have the best electronic properties, which was fortunate because silicon is one of the most plentiful natural substances. These small crystals began replacing the vacuum tubes that had taken up so much space and had required an elaborate cooling system to keep them from overheating.

The other great breakthrough was the development of the integrated circuit, or IC. This was a device that included all the components of an electrical circuit but was made out of one basic material. The basic material that integrated circuits were made of was once again silicon. (In California the place where most of the companies producing ICs were located was called Silicon Valley.)

In the 1960s, the space race between the United States and the Soviet Union required smaller and smaller computers—computers small enough to fit into a spacecraft. Once again necessity spurred a technological leap forward. Smaller and smaller computers required smaller and smaller integrated circuits, or microprocessors, which began to be called chips. By the mid-1960s the number of components per chip was doubling every year, and it was predicted that this trend would continue. (It did, and by 1990 the number of transistors that could be put onto a single chip was 4 million.)

By 1974 the chips had long been small enough to make a personal computer a possibility. But even though a chip that could serve as the central processing unit of a computer could fit on the tip of your little finger, they were still relatively expensive. The chip alone would cost nearly $400, so how could MITS produce a computer for less than that?

MITS was about $400,000 in debt when they had a meeting with their accountant in the summer of 1974. The accountant said, "Ed, we need to shut this thing down. There's no way you can get out of here. You're in such a hole there's no way you can come out of the hole." Having always found technical challenges more interesting than money, Ed Roberts ignored him and went shopping for chips.

Several companies had chips. Motorola had a microprocessor that Roberts considered, and so did Texas Instruments. The Intel Corporation of Silicon Valley had a new chip out, the Intel 8080. That was the one Roberts wanted, but the price was $360. He finally talked Intel into selling him the 8080 chips for $75 apiece. Of course in order to get that price, he had to buy a large volume.

The loan officers at the bank were understandably hesitant about advancing the $65,000 Roberts asked for. They didn't think very many people would buy kits to assemble their own computers. On the other hand, Roberts already owed the bank so much money that they were afraid he would go bankrupt and they wouldn't get paid any of it. They finally decided that if there was a chance he could sell even 200 of the computers, they might get some of their money back. They granted the loan.

Steve Wozniak was a member of the Homebrew Computer Club in 1975. He was one of many who ordered an Altair Computer from Ed Roberts. Wozniak co-founded Apple Computer Company with Steve Jobs in 1976.

Chapter 4

Revolution

Ed Roberts and Bill Yates had the design, they had the Intel 8080 chips and they had a deadline: they had to have a working prototype of their computer delivered to *Popular Electronics* in time for the cover story of the January 1975 issue. The editors called Ed Roberts while they were working on the story to ask him what the name of the computer would be. His reaction was, "Who cares?" which he later admitted showed his naiveté about marketing. He gave the editors the job of coming up with a name.

A few days later Les Solomon called to say that he had asked his 12-year-old daughter Lauren what she thought a good name would be. Lauren was watching *Star Trek.* She picked the name of the star that the starship *Enterprise* was heading for: Altair. "That's a great name," Ed Roberts said. "We'll use that." So they had a name, and they were working frantically on the prototype.

When it was finished, they gave it to Railway Express to deliver to *Popular Electronics.* Roberts was going to fly to New York the next day, but he decided it would be safer to ship it than to trust it to the baggage system of the airline. By sending it Railway Express, which was the UPS of that time, they could insure it. They sent it by their Air Express Service. Unfortunately, it didn't arrive until six months later. The day that MITS shipped the one and only Altair computer, Railway Express went bankrupt and all their operations were shut down. All the packages they had were held for months and months.

At *Popular Electronics* the editors decided to go ahead with the article even without the working prototype of the computer. At MITS they worked frantically to make an actual mockup of a real front panel of the Altair and sent it to *Popular Electronics* to be photographed for their cover. The magazine came out with a cover and an article about a computer that no one but Ed Roberts and Bill Yates had ever actually seen. The readers of *Popular Electronics* didn't know that the picture was a fake.

The day the magazine came out, the telephone at MITS began to ring. It kept ringing. Within a month MITS went from being $400,000 in debt to having a bank balance of $250,000. And the phone kept ringing.

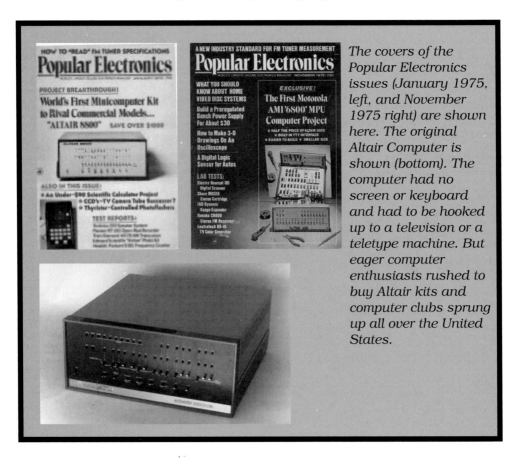

The covers of the Popular Electronics issues (January 1975, left, and November 1975 right) are shown here. The original Altair Computer is shown (bottom). The computer had no screen or keyboard and had to be hooked up to a television or a teletype machine. But eager computer enthusiasts rushed to buy Altair kits and computer clubs sprung up all over the United States.

The Altair didn't look like today's personal computers. The basic kit didn't have a keyboard or a screen. There was no software. Just like the owners of today's computers, the Altair owners had to buy an external screen or a Teletype machine in order to use the computer. But it was possible to use the Altair in a minimal way by using the front panel maintenance switches, which is exactly what many of MITS's eager customers did. The only way to program the Altair was by flipping the switches on its front panel. But as Ted Nelson observed in his book *Computer Lib*, "All this pent-up demand burst forth. It was as though all the galley slaves were suddenly able to jump overboard in life preservers in their own little computers because they were no longer enslaved to the computer center and its bureaucratic mentality."

The two kids from Seattle, Paul Allen and Bill Gates, saw the January 1975 issue of *Popular Electronics* and called Ed Roberts. "They were among about 50 people that got in touch with us," Roberts remembers. "They all had software they wanted to sell us. We finally just said, 'Whoever shows up here first with a working copy will get the contract.'" The contract was to be for programming for the Altair in BASIC, Beginners All-purpose Symbolic Instruction Code, the computer language that would be accepted by the Intel 8080 chip.

Paul Allen showed up at MITS without ever having seen an Altair, but with a paper tape that had a copy of BASIC on it. "We loaded that BASIC in the Altair," Roberts says. "It loaded, came up, said 'OK' and then promptly crashed. But at least it got that far." The next day Allen called Gates and made some modifications on the program over the phone, and the Altair was running BASIC within 24 hours after Paul Allen got to Albuquerque. Ed Roberts hired Allen as the Director of Software. Of course at that time Allen was the entire software department at MITS. The company wasn't very big. But it was going to grow fast.

As the orders came pouring in, Ed Roberts realized that the top priority had to be getting the basic kits into the mail to the people who had ordered them. It took MITS nearly six months to get that under control. One of the worst things that can happen to a small company is overwhelming success. And that's what was happening to MITS.

"There were a lot of things we needed to do," Roberts remembers. "We needed to develop our production facility a lot more. We were selling a lot more assembled units than we were kits. And that was true right from the beginning. Our assembly line was still a calculator-type assembly line. We didn't have any automatic insertion of equipment . . . we didn't have any free capital. Every bit of money that we were making was buying more parts to send out with a bigger order next month. We had more orders the next month, and with a thin margin, we were always behind the power curve."

Ed Roberts and Bill Yates had designed the Altair to be expandable, able to add features and functions. Although the company had plans to produce add-ons for the Altair, and had designed most of them, under the constant crushing pressure of getting their orders out, they couldn't develop other products fast enough to keep up with the demand. All across the country, and particularly in California, computer enthusiasts improvised their own solutions, their own software, and their own add-ons for the Altair.

In early March of 1975, the first meeting of the Homebrew Computer Club was held in a garage in Menlo Park, California. So far about all the Altair could do was flash its lights, but just its existence was enough to fire the creativity of the Homebrew members. They wrote their own programs. They took them to Homebrew meetings and shared them with other members who had Altairs or who had ordered Altairs and were waiting for them to arrive. Before long the club was so large it filled an auditorium at Stanford University. Some of the club's members formed small companies that built add-on devices for the Altair, such as circuit boards to increase the computer's memory. Steve Wozniak was one Homebrew member who was designing and selling circuit boards.

The same thing was happening all over the country. "The basic ground rules for a personal computer from a technical standpoint," Roberts says, "is that it had to be a real, fully operational computer that was fully expandable and at least in principal could do anything that a general-purpose minicomputer of the time could do." Computer clubs were forming to exchange software and home-built add-ons for the Altair. Ed Roberts encouraged the activity with his mobile unit, The Blue Goose, which traveled around the country. The majority of the computer clubs that were formed in the United States were the result of this traveling road show.

When the MITS marketing director suggested that they should have the first Altair Convention in Albuquerque, Ed Roberts' reaction was that the idea was crazy, and that they weren't going to get people to come all the way to Albuquerque. For once Roberts was wrong. Hundreds of computer enthusiasts from all over the country showed up,

Steve Jobs co-founded Apple Computer with Steve Wozniak. Jobs was the marketing genius and Wozniak had the technical talent.

and so did some of the little companies that were creating add-ons and software for the Altair. Roberts remembers that one of the companies, Processor Tech, "identified some of the problems in the Altair and created good products to fix them." This was a typical example of the way the development of the personal computer occurred. It all started with the Altair, but by two or three years later not only companies making other products to use with the Altair, but also computer companies imitating the Altair had sprung up like mushrooms after a rain.

By the end of 1976, MITS had developed the personal computer very nearly to what they are like today. The disks, floppy disks, color graphics all were on the market from MITS. Everything since that time has been refinement, greater sophistication, speed, and lower cost. The basic concepts had all been done by MITS by late 1976. Not very much has changed in the design of personal computer hardware.

In 1977, Ed Roberts sold his company to a large corporation called Pertec. MITS was continuing its rapid growth and by 1977 was selling at the rate of $20 million a year—the rate of sales had gone up every month from the time they started in January 1975. Those figures sound as though Roberts should have been a wealthy man, but he wasn't.

"Pertec had a lot of money and I didn't," he explains. "Unfortunately there was very little profit in those machines. They were being sold for just a tiny little bit over our cost. That was particularly true of the machines that went to dealers. The profit was paper thin."

Roberts sold MITS to Pertec in May of 1977 for $6 million. He was made a division vice president, but nothing in his way of working made it likely that he would be able to endure the corporate way of thinking.

Vice President Roberts wanted to develop a laptop computer. The administration of Pertec didn't even really believe that people needed a desktop computer, Roberts remembers, "and they were sure sure that they didn't need a laptop computer. So I told the guy I worked for, who was an executive vice president, that they were probably right, but I was clearly so wrong that I didn't need to be there, and I resigned. I wasn't mad at anybody. It was just clear that I didn't understand the problem or they didn't understand the problem. We were so far apart that I didn't see any reason to hang around."

Dr. Ed Roberts poses in his office. Visible in the picture is his first electronic calculator and the Altair Computer.

Chapter 5

Doctor Roberts

● ●

By the time Ed Roberts left Albuquerque late in 1977 he had five sons—Edward had been born in 1972 and Martin in 1975. The three older boys were about ready to start high school. Roberts bought a farm in Wheeler County, Georgia. "In rural areas at that time, drugs hadn't really penetrated." Roberts observes, "They've penetrated everywhere now, but at that time I thought it was a better environment for my children, and I still think that is true. I think the experience of living on a farm and having responsibilities was good for them. And they were able to do things that none of their peers in the city could do."

From 1977 to 1982 Roberts farmed, raising soybeans, corn, several hundred head of cattle, and a few hogs. Never one to settle for just one job, Roberts started a software company during the same period, and he wrote some agricultural software. He had a non-competing contract with Pertec, which meant that for five years he couldn't design any hardware. By the time the five-year limit was up, Ed Roberts was in medical school, which was where he had been headed when he graduated from high school nearly 25 years earlier. He had just taken a few side trips along the way.

His daughter, Dawn, was born in 1983. In 1986 he graduated with his M.D. from Mercer University in Macon, Georgia. He did a two-year residency in internal medicine until 1988. "If you practice in a small town," he says, "you're basically a general practitioner no matter what your specialty is. But I was trained as an internist." Dr. Ed Roberts currently has a thriving medical practice in the little town of Cochran, Georgia, which has a population of about 4,500. He has written some medical software, MDplus, to help handle the running of a busy doctor's office. Ed Roberts was inducted into the Consumer Electronics Hall of Fame in 2000 for building the first successful personal computer, the Altair 8800.

His current project is setting up a machine shop. "Everything I do is an avocation," he says. (An avocation is something that someone does because he or she loves doing it, in contrast to a vocation, which is a job that is done primarily to earn money.) "MITS was an avocation. I don't have a vocation. Medicine is an avocation. This machine shop is for fun. There are a number of ideas I'd like to play with."

While Roberts was farming, writing software, and studying medicine, the industry he had started was experiencing explosive growth. About the time he sold MITS to Pertec, Steve Wozniak, who had created some of the first circuit boards to increase Altair's memory, and Steve Jobs were launching their own computer company, Apple. The big computer businesses like IBM and Hewlett-Packard, the ones that had decided personal computers would never sell, changed their minds. They started making and marketing personal computers as fast as they could. Dozens of smaller companies emerged. Some flourished for a while, others failed.

But the changes took place not in the hardware, the design of the computers themselves, but in software. Literally hundreds of software companies, including those Ed Roberts started, created programs for the personal computers. In the beginning of the personal computer revolution, enthusiastic members of computer clubs like the Homebrew Computer Club shared their programs and felt that the software should be free for anyone who wanted to use it.

Bill Gates didn't agree. In 1976, while he was working on BASIC programs for the Altair, he wrote a letter saying that users who copied and used his programs were thieves. His letter was received with hostility by the many computer users who wanted to see programs available free to be used for the public good. Bill Gates and Paul Allen formed a software company they called Microsoft, and Bill Gates has become one of the wealthiest men in the world by being sure that people pay for his company's software.

It is the development of software that has made personal computers available for just about everyone's use. Computers had formerly been used only by specially trained professionals or by enthusiastic hobbyists (called hackers— people who were fascinated with what computers could do). People who have no idea at all how computers work can now use computers. Preschool children use computer programs to learn how to count, or to learn the letters of the alphabet. Retail store owners use computer programs to keep track of their inventories. Private clubs have programs that keep track of their events and of their membership. Students use the Internet to do research for their classes. Writers and editors use word processing programs to publish magazines and books. In fact it is now difficult to find anyone who doesn't use a personal computer either at work or at home or both.

When Dr. Ed Roberts looks back at the former avocation that was MITS and the design, development, and marketing of the first personal computer, he says, "We were naive. I'm talking about at MITS we were naive. From this standpoint—and I think about that a good bit—if someone were to come up to me now and say, 'Why don't we start a company, and what we'll do is we'll develop a computer system. And of course to develop the computer system you have to develop the memory and the input and the output and the printer and the monitor and the keyboard system, and you've got to put all that together. And oh, by the way, you can only have one electrical engineer on this project.'

"And I'd say, 'That's crazy. You can't do that. It isn't doable.' Yet, we did it. But that was just naiveté. But the big advantage young people have over folks that have been around for a while is that they don't know they can't do it. And that's real important if you're going to do something new and creative and exciting. If you know that you can't do it, you'll never do it. But if you don't know that, then there's no telling what you can do."

Ed Roberts has never become as wealthy as Bill Gates, Steve Jobs, or Steve Wozniak. He is not a household name, either. But he has accomplished more in his lifetime than most could ever dream. He was at the forefront of a technological revolution that has only just begun to pay dividends.

Ed Roberts Chronology

1941 born in Miami, Florida

1943 moves with mother to his grandparents' farm in Georgia

1945 moves back to Miami when his father returns from the army, but continues to spend summers in Georgia

1957 builds relay computers while in high school

1958 graduates from high school and begins working in special research program for experimental surgery

1962 marries Joan; enlists in U.S. Air Force; enters electronics school at Lackland Air Force Base, San Antonio, Texas

1963 son Melvin born

1964 son Clark born

1965 attends Oklahoma State University at Stillwater, Oklahoma; son David born

1968 receives electrical engineering degree from Oklahoma State; transfers to special weapons lab in Albuquerque, New Mexico

1969 starts Micro Instrumentation Telemetry Systems, MITS, with two other Air Force officers as partners

1972 discharged from the Air Force; MITS designs and markets a programmable calculator; son Edward born

1975 MITS's Altair, the first personal computer, appears on the cover of the January issue of *Popular Electronics;* son Martin born

1977 sells MITS to Pertec Corporation; buys a farm in Georgia; begins software company

1982 enrolls in medical school at Mercer University in Macon, Georgia

1983 daughter Dawn born

1986 receives M.D. from Mercer University

1988 completes residency in internal medicine; begins medical practice in Cochran, Georgia

2000 inducted into the Consumer Electronics Hall of Fame

Computer Timeline

5000 B.C. abacus in use

1621 A.D. commercial version of slide rule available

1644 Blaise Pascal invents the first calculating machine

1679 Gottfried Leibniz perfects binary system of notation

1775 Charles Stanhope develops his calculating machine

1801	Joseph-Marie Jacquard invents punch cards
1834	Charles Babbage begins work on his Difference Engine and Analytic Engine, the first general-purpose computer
1873	Philo Remington manufactures the first typewriters
1885	William Burroughs patents his first adding machine
1889	Hollerith Electric Tabulating System adopted for the 1890 U.S. Census
1924	International Business Machines (IBM) formed from Hollerith's Tabulating Machine Co.'s successor, Computer-Tabulating-Recording Co.
1936	Konrad Zuse develops electromechanical calculator that uses binary instead of decimal system
1943	Colossus developed in England to decode German encryption system used throughout World War II
1944	Harvard Mark I, inspired by Babbage's calculating engines and created by IBM, is dedicated at Harvard
1945	the ENIAC (Electronic Numerical Integrator and Computer) completed by John W. Mauchly and J. Presper Eckert at the Moore School of Electrical Engineering; John von Neumann writes report on EDVAC (Electronic Discrete Variable Automatic Computer)
1948	transistor invented
1949	EDSAC (Electronic Delay Storage Automatic Calculator) designed by Maurice Wilkes begins operating at Cambridge in England
1960	IBM 1401, first transistor computer, placed on market; Digital Equipment Corporation (DEC) markets its minicomputer PDP-1
1965	DEC produces PDP-8, the first minicomputer to exploit integrated circuits
1975	the Altair 8800, the first personal computer, marketed by MITS
1976	Microsoft formed by Bill Gates and Paul Allen, followed by many other software companies
1977	Tandy, Apple, Commodore, and other personal computer manufacturers enter the market
1983	Internet as it is today is born when computer network splits into military and civilian sectors
1989	World Wide Web is developed
1995	Sun Microsystems releases an internet programming language called Java
2002	Electronics giant Hewlett-Packard and Compaq Corporation merge

Further Reading

Books For Young Readers

Borman, Jami Lynne. *Computer Dictionary for Kids.* New York: Barrons, 1995.

Graham, Ian. *How-It-Works: Computers.* New York: Gloucester Press, 1992.

Greene, Laura. *Computer Pioneers.* London: Franklin Watts, 1985.

Williams, Brian. *Computers.* Crystal Lake, IL: Heinemann Library, 2001.

Adult Books

Campbell-Kelly, Martin, and William Osprey. *Computer: A History of the Information Machine.* New York: Basic Books, 1996.

Freiberger, Paul, and Michael Swaine. *Fire in the Valley: The Making of the Personal Computer.* New York: McGraw-Hill, 1999.

Palfreman, Jon, and Daron Swade. *The Dream Machine: Exploring the Computer Age.* London: BBC Books, 1991.

Web Sites

A Science Odyssey: People and Discoveries
www.pbs.org/wgbh/aso/databank/entries/dt75co.html

History of Computer Science
www.thestudy.qc.ca/Students/History/Roberts/About%20Ed%20Roberts.html

Ed Roberts Interview with *Historically Brewed* Magazine
exo.com/~wts/mits0011.HTM

Excerpt from *Fire in the Valley*
www.fireinthevalley.com/fitv_book5.html

Glossary of Terms

abacus: a device for calculating using sliding counters along rods or in grooves

BASIC: an acronym for Beginners All-purpose Symbolic Instruction Code, a simple programming language.

binary system: a counting system based on only two numbers, zero and one.

capacitor: a device for storing an electrical charge.

decimal system: the traditional 10-number (0–9) counting system.

digital: using discrete units, or digits, as opposed to continuous units.

hardware: the physical parts of a computer system.

integrated circuit (IC): a small piece of semiconductor material that includes a complete electronic circuit. Also referred to as a chip.

keyboard: a section of a computer system that looks like a typewriter, with letters, numbers, and other symbols.

laptop computer: a computer with a built-in screen and keyboard small enough to be carried and used on the lap.

mainframe computer: a very large, very fast, and very expensive computer that can be used by hundreds of people at the same time, running many different programs.

microcomputer: the more technical name for a personal computer.

microprocessor: the chips, or ICs, that contain a computer's master control circuit, the central processing unit, or CPU.

minicomputer: a computer smaller than a mainframe but larger than a personal computer that can run many programs at the same time.

program: the instructions that tell a computer what activity to perform.

relay: an electromechanical switching device used in telephone exchanges and in some early computers.

resistor: an electrical component that impedes the flow of electric current in a circuit.

silicon: a hard, dark gray chemical element used in electronics.

software: the programs run by a computer system.

transistor: a small electrical device, usually made of silicon, that controls the flow of an electrical current.

vacuum tube: a sealed glass tube with metal plates inside that control the movements of electrons emitted from a heated filament; also called a valve.

Index